MW00736768

Come Hang Out With Me Mandalas and Poetry The Poet LaFe

A Book of Poems & Symbolic Drawings

by

Ophelia J. Thompson

Book title is a Haiku - Senryu
Front cover sketch by M.J. Thomas

This project is supported in part by a grant from
The Arts Commission of Greater Toledo

FOR ADDITIONAL INFORMATION

If you would like information regarding:

___ Author's performances (times, dates and places).
___ Ordering copies of this book.
___ Places to purchase copies of this book.
___ Book signings and other public appearances.
___ Workshops (times, dates and places).

Contact the author at: **The Poet LaFe**
P.O. Box 672
Perrysburg, Ohio 43552-0672

Phone: 419-666-8579

Email addresses: ojst47@hotmail .com
EDGART522@aol .com

Visit website at: http://www.shider.com/lafe/index.htm

*This book will be available on Tape/CD in the fall of 2003.

~~~~~~

International Standard Book Number 0-9724874-0-9

Printed in Perrysburg, Ohio by Welch Publishing Co.

First Printing October, 2002.

TABLE OF CONTENTS

III. **Personal Growth Poems**

IV. **Relationship Poems**

BASIC ACKNOWLEDGMENT

God of my understanding, androgyny, is neither He nor She;
Him or Her, whatever you prefer.
This God of every race I can see in your face.
For me, God can be, whatever I can see;
even when I cannot see, still God can be.

PERSONAL PRAYER POEM

God of my understanding, "I do,"
adore, honor and glorify You,
praise Your names and thank You too.

Your names and forms to be revered,
until to me You have appeared.
I salute You here in time,
as You dwell within my heart and mind.

I offer up praise and glory,
and respect each Holy story.
My Higher Power, You are known
God Almighty on Your throne.

Everlasting Prince of Peace,
prayer and praise must never cease.
Lord, Savior, Jesus the Christ,
early Christian sacrifice.

Holy Ghost sent to earth,
Spirit of God in human birth.
Brahma, Siva and Vishnu,
other ancient forms of You.

Horus, the Tao, the Absolute,
Pan playing the ancient flute.
Isis and Osiris, too,
Apollo and Father Zeus.

The Great Mother, Hathor,
Gautama, the Buddha.
The one Great Spirit in earth and air,
Great Ultimate, God is everywhere.

Known to many as Allah,
others call You Jehovah.
Yahweh is another name,
Your presence on earth to proclaim.

The name of every deity,
precious and valuable to me.
Excluding none, all refer
to each his own, as each prefer.

Forms and names used by man,
trying so hard to understand.
Unknowable truth in abstraction,
creating God, human reaction.

Trying so hard to be discrete,
bringing abstract into concrete.
Concretization of God, impossible task,
vocation of man, present and past.

OTHER ACKNOWLEDGEMENTS

I owe a debt of gratitude to the following individuals, organizations, institutions and business establishments; for each in some way played a significant role in helping, encouraging and/or inspiring me to begin, work on and complete this project.

Cheryl Catlin
M.J. Thomas
Edgar Thompson
Isaac Shider, Sr.
Corinthia Parker
Rev. Albert Reed
Dr. Jerry Deburin
Ann Redmond
Art "Thunder" Vaughn
Collette Jacobs
Thelma Smith
Mildred Clark
Anna Scurles
Edward Carr
Judy Lee
Sandra Davis
Bret Collins
Eldora Cosby (Mom)
Marty Campbell
Joyce Brown
Susan Megyesi
Harriet Allen
Margie Heckman
Ruth Whittle

Arts Commission of Greater Toledo
Minstrel Soup (Poetry Olympics)
Murphy's Place
The Toledo Blade
Unity Church
First Antioch Church
Cherry School
Glenwood School
McKinley School
The City Paper
New Century Club
Step Up Toledo
The In Zone
NW Ohio Writer's Forum
Toledo-Lucas County Library
Mott & Sanger Branches
Ramona Collins
Susie Crite (Cousin)
Brewed Awakenings
Dorothy Day
Tom Singleton
Kathy Gregory
The Poet Dorfay
Bertha Huckaby

*Although this list is rather long, I know I've missed a few,
but deep within my heart and soul, I included you.
Because you chose this book, your name goes on this line,
As I share a part of me, the pleasure is all mine.

Thank You!

Mattie Bacon
(Your Name Here)

Forever **"BIGMAMA"**
1895-1997
Amy Lurry-McCloud

Sketch by Judy Lee

DEDICATIONS

This book is dedicated to three departed souls,
whose memories shine for me like purest gold.

Amy Lurry McCloud

April15, 1895 - July 5, 1997

…she always was and always will be
my "Big Mama"

I honor my grandmother, Amy McCloud,
daughter of slaves, a woman so proud.
Our lives intertwined since the day of my birth,
a great influence upon my journey here on earth.

Margaret Smith

August 9, 1897 - February 20, 1996

…she always was and always will be
my "Cousin Margaret"

I honor and commemorate,
a woman, to me, who was so great.
Just a short time before she died, she spoke to me of angels by her side.

Morris D. Davis, III

July 8, 1947 - July 23, 2001

…. who always was and always will be
"Bugs"

Mystical, majestic memories
of a marvelously magnificent man.
A friendship unique and rare,
few will understand.

THE POET IN ME

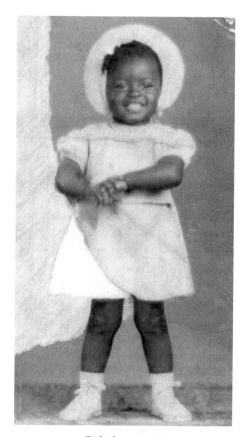

Ophelia, Age 2

Now this is a picture of the Poet LaFe,
she writes a lot of my poetry;
whatever I do, wherever I may be,
she is always within me.

When I was in bondage, she was free,
guided me towards sobriety;
she lets nothing in life get her down,
she has a smile to counter every frown.

I must never lose touch with my inner child,
but allow her to surface for a little while;
she always was and always will be,

The Poet LaFe

POEM OF INTRODUCTION

(Reflections of Human Imperfections)

These poems are most revealing, expressions of what I was feeling; I hope for you they are appealing, and for your soul, spiritual healing.

In this book I will share with you, a little bit of me, and what I do; as I follow a sacred vocation, after thirty years in public education.

To date I have written over **one thousand three hundred sixty-five** poems, several I sing and call them songs; they fall roughly into **forty** categories, my life, my place in this human story.

I've selected **five** categories to share with you; of my many poems, I picked **one hundred two**.

Fifteen are related to my **career**, experiences and memories I hold dear.

Of my **inspirational** poems, there are **twenty-two**; in difficult times, they brought me through.

On **personal growth**, there are **twenty-five**, I am thankful just to be alive.

Twenty-five about **relationship**, where it is so easy to, "flip the script."

Fifteen relate to **ethnicity**, the struggle goes on; we want to be free.

Culture and **gender** intertwined, freedom begins in the mind.

Seven Mandalas from my collection, placed at the beginning and end of each section.

More than **six hundred** Mandalas, I have drawn; revealed to me things I had not known.

A glimpse of the future – be on the look, for the audio version of this book.

The Author

Education

my

Sacred

Vocation

I
career related

Details

TEACHER, "ARE YOU THERE?"

Impostor! Where is my teacher?
Are you a dream or a creature feature?
O Yes! I remember, O Yes, I do
for I once had a teacher just like you;
and I despised her through and through.

Arrogant and snobbish, no feelings inside;
at least, not for me, was she willing to provide.
She gave facts and figures, words and sound;
but in her body, not a caring bone could be found.

Every time I would see her, my stomach turned.
Trying to accept her, I had to learn.
'Though I could not understand, why she did not care;
she cared for the other kids who were there.

"Why doesn't she like me?" I use to ask.
No matter what, she would make me last.
Now, seeing you (just like her) is very hard,
although, I know that there is a reward.

I had to succeed and prove her wrong,
I knew in my heart I had a song;
although she tried to make me think,
that I was a "zero" each time she blinked.

I knew that a teacher I had to be,
to be there for kids just like me.
Kids unloved, from families unlearned,
facing the teacher who makes the stomach turn.

I learned from that teacher, how not to be,
and through caring teachers, I found the key.
It is more than just your A-B-C's,
"number your paper," and "be quiet please."
It is more about, "Do you really care?"
And for the kids, teacher, "Are you there?"

PORTRAIT OF AN EFFECTIVE TEACHER

An effective teacher is not hard to find,
yet rare, for each is one of a kind.
This may sound like a paradox,
an effective teacher can't be placed in a box.

You are blessed when this teacher shares with you.
You'll know exactly what you have to do.
You cannot explain just what you feel,
but you know somehow this teacher is real.

You may not agree with all that they do,
but you know they are doing what is best for you.
It may take some time for you to realize,
why an effective teacher will not compromise.

This teacher stands firm on what is right.
When necessary will stand up and fight.
Constantly going that extra mile,
willingly doing it with a smile.

Never waiting for a pat on the back.
Making decisions that are based on fact.
This teacher has a heart that is pure,
that makes you feel safe and secure.

You know that this teacher cares about you,
and is concerned about the things you do.
This teacher may be a he or a she,
who sets the example of how we should be.

This teacher has a good attitude,
and is usually in a pretty good mood.
Resolves conflict without being rude,
positively affecting our attitudes.

I could go on and on you see,
for this is the kind of teacher I tried to be;
because the example had been set for me,
by teachers who helped me through puberty.

A teacher can be a blessing in life,
or one who causes pain and strife;
but an effective teacher inspires us to be,
the best in life that we can be.

SOME THINGS DON'T CHANGE

There were teachers I loved as a kid,
so many wonderful things they did;
they encouraged me in every way they could,
they taught me to differentiate bad from good.

There were also those I did not like,
they only disciplined out of spite.
They were always busy, "no time for you,"
they were mean and hateful and selfish too.

When I decided a teacher to be,
there was only one role model for me.
The teachers that I loved so well,
not the ones who made school a living hell.

Now I am a school administrator,
sometimes I feel like a moderator;
for parents, kids and teachers
many have the very same features.

Of people from my own childhood,
some of them bad, some of them good;
some things in life don't seem to change,
like people looking for someone else to blame.

It seems that teachers don't really change,
only their faces, appearance and names.
Parents and kids too, are pretty much the same
only the circumstances have been rearranged.

Now here I am some thirty years later,
playing the role of mediator,
examining opposing points-of-view,
in this day of litigation where people sue.

The problem is my point-of-view,
where my main concern in all I do,
is to choose what is best for our youth,
and encourage them to value and seek for truth.

LITTLE PEOPLE
(Children)

Working with little people
will truly keep you straight,
for without malice, they know how,
the ego to deflate.

They will speak the truth
without any provocation,
and bring your ego down
in total mutilation.

They don't intend to hurt,
they just call out what is seen,
sometimes it hits so hard
we think they are being mean.

But the truth of the matter is
their spirits are free.
They're not hung up by society's
mass hypocrisy.

So we dedicate ourselves
to screw them up real bad.
What we do to our kids
is very, very sad.

We role model big lies,
and hide out from the truth.
Then turn around and criticize
the behavior of our youth.

I love little people,
and all they have to give.
If we but pay attention,
they role model how to live.

CHILDREN ARE SO IMPORTANT

Whether or not I get elected,
is neither here nor there,
it is for our children,
particularly that I care.

All of the unions,
the cabinet, expanded too,
have far more privileges
than we are entitled to.

We have created a system
where adults get everything,
that, "children are so important,"
is just the song we sing.

They have no vote
and really have no rights,
yet we cast them in the middle
of our political fights.

I call it like I see it
from the inside out,
and children are not the main focus
of what we are about.

Let us call a spade a spade,
this game is about power,
and more dollars to be earned,
for less work by the hour.

Planning and implementation,
we hold in our hand,
but when things don't turn out right,
we blame the other man.

All the time we spend planning,
in the middle of the school day;
could be spent with kids,
we could plan another way.

With more adult supervision
less the kids could roam,
then we could do our planning
while the kids are at home.

This system we've created,
frankly is full of shit,
while the buck is passed,
on our asses we sit.

Sitting around complaining
about darn near everything,
but, "children are so important"
that's the song we sing.

YES.YES..YES...TO THE PRESS

You can read for yourself, what you see
then get an interpretation from me.
The interpretation that I give,
relates specifically to how I live.
Don't ask me about anyone else,
for I can only speak for myself.
There are things I do not know,
but I do know, where to go.

I seek help down on my knees.
Who do you think I seek to please?
I know where the answers lie,
I'll seek them there 'til the day I die.

Do you want to know about me,
and the vision for children that I see?
I'll be glad to spell it out,
without hesitation reluctance or doubt.

"I see school as a special place,
where children learn about the human race;
in all of its vast variety,
this is the vision that I see.

I see school as a haven of rest,
from a world of confusion and craziness.
A place of love where kids can go,
to learn the things they need to know.

I see school as a happy place,
full of love, full of grace.
Here is my humble confession,
education is a great profession."

Yes, there are problems we seek to solve,
solutions do not just evolve.
In failures we seek to do our best,
no, we don't always pass the test.

But everyday we hang in there,
providing service with love and care;
and when we have given our very best,
'A' plus we get on the final test!

YES.YES..YES...TO THE PRESS

Y
E
S
.

Y
E
S
.
.

Y
E
S
.
.
.

T
O

T
H
E

P
R
E
S
S

FIND THE BETTER WAY

My observations, in education
bring to me, great frustrations;
but a poem and laughter each and everyday,
helps to keep insanity away.

Good teachers come and good teachers go,
but you'll find a few bad ones this I know.
From the bitchiest witch to the classroom queen,
good teachers, bad teacher and all in between.

Many take pride in doing the right thing,
but some complain, are hateful and mean.
A few cry, "perfection," they can do no wrong,
while many work hard helping children belong.

Most love kids and express gratitude,
but a few of them have bad attitudes.
In every school, you will find,
there are teachers of both kinds.

Hallelujah! The bad ones are few,
but they negatively affect what the good ones do.
Try to hold them accountable for the children's sake,
from a dark nightmare, you will not escape.

The grievance process always rules them right.
Is it really worth it just to lose the fight?
So, in every matter they reign supreme,
crying, "file a grievance" for darn near everything.

I've seen favoritism for friend over foe.
Thank goodness there is fairness, some places you go.
Thank God for teachers who love their job,
around the "lounge of gossip," they refuse to hobnob.

They go the extra mile to get the job done,
and find working with children lots and lots of fun.
Who will take the lead, who will take a stand,
to make this system work and find a better plan?

The greatest challenge facing educators today,
in restructuring our schools, is to find a better way.
A way to improve on what we have achieved,
without destroying the principles in which we believe.

THE SOURCE

The children have the answers, if we but pay attention,
facilitate and operate, within their dimension.

When we get together, to try and figure them out,
they already know what we are all about.

They know without a doubt, that we are full of shit,
talking a good game, but do our words and actions fit?

We are the ones behind the eight ball,
yet everyday we pretend, that we know it all.

Can we admit, we are the ones ailing,
or keep on blaming kids, as the ones who are failing?

Yes! There are answers, we don't want to face;
we made the error, in setting the pace.

Now we want to change in the middle of the game,
while steadily trying to keep things the same.

The children are confused, "What the hell." they say,
all this crazy talk about some mythic judgment day.

When many live in hell, every single day,
joining gangs to them, seems a better way.

Who created their hell? Surely they did not.
What we have given them, is all that they have got.

Listen to the children, what they have to say.
Who said, "a little child, can surely lead the way."

OPINIONS
(Respecting Differences)

Don't shove your shit down my throat,
causing me to gag and choke.

You are free to do your thing,
but I can't use the shit you bring.

I think you have lost your mind,
trying to put me in a double bind.

Express your opinion, you have that right,
but don't limit me to your narrow sight.

'Cause baby, I have an opinion too,
and I don't happen to agree with you.

Love from me is not earned,
behavior comes from what is learned.

No matter what some kids do,
they'll not get any love from you.

That's your business and that's all right,
but loving these children is my life long plight.

You can't tell me whom to hug,
even when you it bugs.

I'm not perfect but I work hard,
and damn sure know how to do my job.

You don't like how I operate,
I think you are a few years late.

Your opinion I appreciate,
and I will even contemplate.

But kiss your ass I'll not do,
or sacrifice one child for you.

SCHEDULED TO STAY

I am pissed off enough
to write a thousand poems,
and hurting bad enough
to sing a sad blues song.

I am ticked off enough
to cuss somebody out.
I know deep in my soul
what this is all about.

I am highly discouraged
with many who work with me,
and thoroughly disgusted
with many things I see.

My curriculum
is to work it through,
and find a better way
to do the things I do.

I know I have to stay,
although I want to go.
I have much to write
as I come to know.

TEACHERS CAN BE

Teachers can be angels of light,
beings of love - shining so bright,
diamonds rare - knowledge to share,
living examples of those who care.

To think they all fulfill this role,
with hearts of gold and pureness of soul,
is an unrealistic but beautiful thought,
that teachers would always do, as they ought.

Teachers can be bearers of good,
when they do what they should.
Givers of love all the day long,
spinners of tales and singers of songs.

This would be nice, this would be right
to move us from darkness in the light.
Today I am not so very wise,
when frustrated I tend to criticize.

"Objective?" it seems I cannot be,
as teachers reflect the "shadow" in me.
I'll keep looking for things that are good,
and doing the things I know that I should.

Maybe by being the best I can be,
reflecting the good things that I see,
loving the "shadow" that lives in me,
I'll inspire the good things that
        "teachers can be."

DIFFERENT MOTIVES

(What Are We About?)

We come to the inner city
with motives of our own,
some to help the children
from poor and broken homes.

Some are "A" number one,
standing tall among the very best,
while others are incompetent
they can't pass the test.

Some come to stay
while others come to play.
Many come bringing life
while others come bringing strife.

But some have no skills,
just love to criticize,
judgingly they try to punish,
as they analyze.

We each should examine self
and, "to thine own self be true,"
face the real, true motives
behind the things we do.

Upon self-evaluation
in this field of education,
by divine call
this is my sacred vocation.

I challenge you to look,
your motives to check out,
and honor what you find,
what are we about?

Others come because
there is no place else to go,
and they need a "job"
little else do they know.

They don't know a damn thing,
and are not willing to learn.
They're satisfied as children's lives
go up in smoke, crash and burn.

Many more are creative,
miracle workers they are,
because of their commitment,
many children will go far.

Some even fool themselves,
claiming that they care,
but when the deal is done,
the kids don't have a prayer.

When I find myself the critic
of everybody else,
it is time to take a serious look
deep within myself.

As I look and see
what my motives are,
I can see every child
as a bright and shining star.

EDUCATOR

I AM an educator and very proud to be,
the bearer of a living torch, for this society.
I AM NOT a politician and DO NOT wish to be,
hypocrisy is not for me; I call exactly what I see.

Sometimes I am right, at other times I am wrong,
often times I express myself, in a poem or in a song.
Everything that happens is for the good of all,
many times it forces us to seek the higher call.

My God, let me start seeking, what I need to do
where I need to be, while I am going through.
Lead me and guide me, to my place of bliss
for the message meant for me, I don't want to miss.

I AM in a battle; yes, the war is on,
lead me to a hiding place, for all of my strength is gone.
I AM depleted; beat down to the bone,
but there are lots of others here, I am not alone.

God is my strength, She is with me everyday,
She is the confidence in every word I say.
Though the road gets rough, She is my guiding light.
I'll just keep on holding on, to what I know is right.

    *God is neither "He" nor "She,"
      God for me - androgyny.

THE MESSAGE LIVES ON

Even when the messenger is stoned,
truth in the message tends to live on.

> A martyr some are called to be,
> thus the captive can be set free.

Captivity of mind body or soul,
demands liberation as truth is told.

> Truth as it relates to public education,
> daily demands public liberation.

Many in charge, have no vision
apparent in each major decision.

> They know all about punishment,
> versus providing a safe environment.

Of fair and natural consequence,
where learning from each incident,
is not left to chance but Providence.

> A system of antagonism has been created,
> where hate and folly are compensated.

There is no value on dignity,
the system has become a catastrophe.

> We're asked to admire the emperor's new clothes,
> when it's plain to see that the emperor is exposed.

The punishment model is a model of violence,
where victims are often threatened into silence.

> What Dr. King taught was truth and proof,
> oppression and violence have ruined our youth.

"Educate the best and suspend the rest,
place the focus on proficiency and psychological test."

> Who cares or believes that character counts?
> The big concern is the dollar amount.

You must sell your soul to get on board,
a price that too many are willing to afford.

> It has little to do with qualification,
> background experience or education.

It truly is a case of whom you know,
where you hang out and where you go.

> choose to trust in a Power that is greater than I,
> therefore, I understand and don't even ask why.

"The message," "the truth," is plain to see
and I thank God just for being "me!"

GONE

Dear retirement year,
I am tired and rest is near,
let me out of here.

Nothing left to say,
will not stay another day,
I am on my way.

Fifty-two I quit,
so fed up with the bull shit,
children took the hit.

No hesitation.
By prayer and meditation.
No reservations.

Celebrate in glee,
release from insanity,
freedom to be me.

Poet - many fears,
in limbo for thirty years,
shed so many tears.

It's all over now,
poetic law does allow,
with time to learn how.

Things from near and far,
cards, a clock, a coat, a car,
sober at a bar.

*Each stanza a Haiku (technically a Senryu – no reference to a season.)

II
inspirational

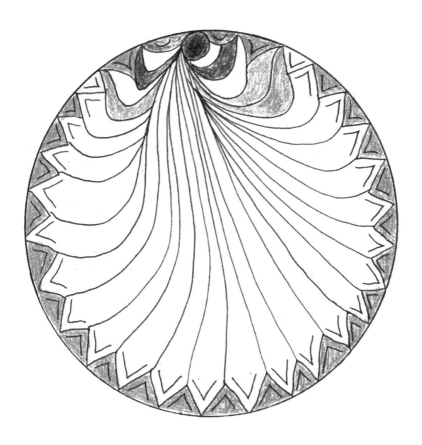

Angel Dance

TIME

There is a time to talk,
and there is a time to walk.
When there is nothing left to say,
we must learn to walk away.

There is a time to learn,
and there is a time to turn.
When there is no more to learn,
our attention we must turn.

Every end
brings a new beginning.
It may seem that we are losing,
but actually we are winning.

There is a time to be glad,
and there are times we are sad.
At times we'll have to cry,
makes us think we want to die.

But when the rain stops falling,
we see the bright sunshine,
then we see our calling,
and how all things work in time.

TIMES OF DEEP DEPRESSION

In times of deep depression,
life may seem dark and dim,
you sometimes feel insecure,
like you are hanging out on a limb.

If you keep holding on,
sooner or later things will change.
Try not to be impatient,
sometimes life can be strange.

We live in 'doubt' and 'hope,'
conflicts in our soul,
then through the refining fire,
we come forth as purest gold.

The bringing forth of life,
requires a lot of pain.
The final results is witness,
that suffering is not in vain.

Even miscarriage of justice,
abortion of good ideas,
cannot be counted as loss,
just part of our natural fears.

We have to look within ourselves,
to overcome these fears,
and realize there is much relief,
in the shedding of our tears.

Depression is temporary,
Thank God it does not last.
We can think of our depression,
as a thing of the past.

Looking towards the future,
is always bright to me,
for the future holds
great possibilities.

YOUR FUTURE

Devise a scheme.
Pursue your dream.
Your future should not be left
to anybody else.

Don't allow another's mistake
to determine your fate.
Take control.
Free your soul.

Use your mind
all of the time.
Don't fool around
and play the clown.

Make a fuss.
Be serious.
Follow your head
then you'll be led.

Follow your heart
because it's smart.
Take advice.
Pay the price.

Listen well.
Skills for sell.
Life is a test.
Do your best.

There is much to gain.
There is much to lose.
Don't be a fool,
follow the rule.

There is always something to earn,
just wait until your turn.
Spend your life in quest
of the very best.

In life the world is the school,
where we learn to live the "golden rule,"
and when we can learn no more,
life abruptly shuts the door.

CHANGE YOURSELF

Yes! I am alive today!
My philosophy is to live and let live.
Amidst the growing pains of life,
we all have something to give.

You may not clearly understand
the position of every man,
but beyond human knowledge,
there is a divine plan.

If you choose to stereotype
and limit what you believe,
you will also limit in life,
what you can achieve.

To think that one or a few
truly represents a whole,
is a narrow point-of-view,
one that is very old.

So when you set out to change the world,
you must begin with yourself.
You can motivate, inspire, and do well,
but you will not change anyone else.

Others may change because of your
influence in their lives,
but it is up to them to
or not to compromise.

When you see yourself in another,
it is an awful thing to see.
It is usually that part of you,
that you are trying not to be.

If you truly want to know yourself,
the true authentic you,
take a look at someone else,
who brings out the worst in you.

Spend time analyzing,
why they get on your nerve.
Be dishonest with yourself,
and you'll throw yourself a curve.

Spend time meditating,
on how they get to you,
and you will learn more about yourself,
and what you need to do.

21

JUST NEED SOME REST

Are you restless, tired, pushing hard,
some behaviors not very smart?
Like doing drugs, and drinking more,
Abusing your body like a whore.

Is something bugging you and won't go away,
the same old 'jones' everyday?
Something within, tearing you apart,
gaining control is very hard.

Maybe you just need some rest,
for life is the ultimate test.
It is also a reason to celebrate,
when with the earth you can relate.

Why work so hard and push yourself?
When all is gone there is nothing left.
Then what will you do, can you now see?
Your 'being' yearns, it wants to be free.

The unconscious brings freedom to us,
for it is in God, we must trust.
Along the way, take time to rest
look to the hills, you are already blessed.

WORLD VIEW

Look at how you view the world,
what is your point-of-view?
For how you view the world
determines what you will do.

If you look to anyone else
to make things right for you;
you will see disappointment,
in your worldview.

You must take what you have
and do the best you can,
you'll find peace and satisfaction,
when this you understand.

There is no perfect world,
check your worldview;
for if perfection is what you seek,
disappointment waits for you.

When the happiness that you seek,
is somewhere outside yourself;
you'll come to the end of your life,
without happiness or anything else.

"If" this, and "if" that
won't help you find success.
You must take what you have
and do your very best.

You are not better off,
or worse than anyone else.
Accept your challenge in life,
take your talents off the shelf.

Take your emotions
and make them work for you.
Don't make excuses,
do what you need to do.

You can find a way,
to get the job done;
put things in prospective,
it really can be fun.

Remember
there is a place for you,
find your place in life,
and do what you have to do.

HELLISH DEPRESSION

Will I ever learn,
when life gets me down,
if I but trust in God,
things will get turned around?

Hellish depression
is just temporary,
for my spiritual growth
it has proven necessary.

There is great value in waiting,
for patience is a virtue;
it helps to focus life,
on things that are true.

Afraid to face change,
change revealed in time;
overwhelmed by life's corrections,
so much truth to find.

The things that we desire most,
bring the greatest pain.
When we face the truth about ourselves,
we can be very vain.

The fear of being rejected,
with low self-esteem;
longing for recognition,
just wanting to be seen.

Seen and recognized,
by significant others,
acceptance and appreciation,
from sisters and brothers.

Love is a great need,
received and given.
The desire to find love,
can cause us to be driven.

Right up to the edge
of time, into eternity;
for love is stronger than death,
we can plainly see.

OPPORTUNITY TODAY

Each problem, each concern
      is an opportunity to learn,
            how to cope and deal
                  and face what we feel.

We cannot change
      nor rearrange,
            things of yesterday
                  by what we do or say.

Tomorrow and tomorrow
      holds great joy and sorrow.
            It's today that we live
                  to give what we must give.

To worry about tomorrow
      only brings pain and sorrow,
            if we let it take away
                  the joys of today.

Choose good things from the past
      as memories to last.
            Let our lives today
                  be built on yesterday.

Today let us see
      opportunity,
            to work problems out
                  work through pain and doubt.

Let us discern
      legitimate concern.
            See what is real
                  then do God's will.

For it is the will of God
      revealed to the heart,
            our full guarantee
                  of life eternally.

EMOTE

You can't lose what you've never had,
the truth of it all is very sad.

Loves lost, never were,
we don't know what we prefer.

Self-deception, false pretense,
the consequence is self-defense.

Wanting, needing, grabbing more,
weaved in time, we cannot soar.

No matter what we choose,
case closed, we lose.

For all have been abused,
and all can be accused.

Reality is a big liar,
we must soar and move up higher.

Emotions burn hot, like a fire
but knowledge is what we must acquire.

Emotions left out of control,
can destroy the immortal soul.

Cognition trained, takes control,
guides emotional energies of the soul.

Pure and priceless, creating life,
born of misery, pain and strife.

Emote, think and meditate.
wherever you are, it is not too late.

You will know what to do,
for the whole universe is you.

EVERYTHING

I am the universe, the universe is me,
a spiritual being bound and free.
I am the cosmos, the cosmos is me
imagination and reality.

I am the beginning, the end,
an enemy, a friend.
I am darkness, I am light,
day and night.

I am good, I am bad,
happy and sad,
right or wrong,
I am a song.

I am Adam, I am Eve,
all that I believe,
I am faith, I am doubt,
a whisper, a shout.

I am here, I am there;
I am everywhere.
I am up, I am down,
a smile and a frown.

I am you, I am me,
all that I can be.
I am young, I am old,
silver and gold.

I have aged, I am youth,
a lie and the truth.
I am dull, I am bright,
black and white.

I am rich, I am poor;
I need nothing, I need more.
I'm a boy, I'm a girl,
co-existing in the world.

I am low, I am high,
the sea and the sky.
I am soft, I am loud;
I am humble, I am proud.

I'm slim,
I'm fat,
a thermostat.

I'm smart,
I am dumb,
a gentleman, a bum.

I'm a woman,
I'm a man.
I can sit,
I can stand.

I'm occult,
I'm religion,
I am a decision.

I'm an image,
I'm a sound;
I am flat,
I am round.

I'm a thought,
I am matter;
I am silence,
I am chatter.

I create,
I destroy;
I lay off,
I employ.

I am law,
I am crime;
I am space in time.

I am all in one,
and one in all;
I am the answer,
I am the call.

Let me speak,
I will sing,
I am everything.

THE IGNORANT I

I am ignorant, but I want to know;
and I am learning where to go.
The place of inspiration,
is the place of information.

When I listen, I learn
concentrate and discern;
I see what I can be,
when I look inside of me.

I taste and I smell
my soul is not for sale;
I touch and I feel,
nothing is for real.

I sing and I cling
to almost everything.
In this present time,
I am stretching out my mind.

I run a kind of race,
as I occupy my place;
I am a woman of passion
creating my own fashion.

Love I have known,
since the time I left home.
Who cares what I feel,
when nothing is for real?

I have loved, I have lost;
I have paid the cost.
I surrender, I give in;
I've been born again.

I have given, I have received;
I've been blessed and deceived.
I know nothing, I know all;
I had to rise before the fall.

Now, ignorant I stand,
holding out my hand.
"The ignorant I"
Asking why?

BEWARE!

I love hearing nice things when they are said,
expressed in love or resentment and dread;
beware when nice things are said about you,
don't let them control the things you do.

Inspiration must come from deep within.
Beware! Hypocrisy is a false friend.
Motivation must come from inside oneself,
it will not last from any place else.

All that you seek and all that you find,
are the things that bring peace of mind;
when you seek the answer outside yourself,
you look to the right then to the left.

You'll come full circle to where the answers lie,
within the land of the sweet bye and bye;
life should not be spent knee deep in bullshit,
if it is not important, then you should quit.

Whatever you seek, you will find;
seeking is not a waste of time.
You will have to seek beyond your youth,
if in this life you are to find the truth.

GREAT COSMIC UNIVERSAL VOICE

One day I turned on a light,
and I could hardly tell;
then when the darkness came,
the light made all things well.
They are interdependent,
both must exist;
so I stopped trying to do away
with the vast darkness.

If you are in heaven,
you should be content;
hell is not something
you need to resent.
For as long as there is heaven,
there will be hell;
as long as things are bought,
there will be things to sell.

Contrast and opposites
will always exist.
This you will grasp
on your journey to the abyss.

What is a smile without a frown?
Without up there is no down.
We contrast happiness with things sad,
then compare goodness with what we call bad.

Without evil there would be no choice.
Against silence, we lift our voice.
In the dead of winter, we long for spring,
to feel the warmth and hear the birds sing.

It is in pain that we appreciate health,
and by poverty we define wealth.
Can one decide or choose for another?
Are we keepers of our sisters and brothers?

Many say, "There is just one way,"
but God gives us choice;
each must listen to recognize,
the great cosmic universal voice.

A SPIRITUAL BLEND

You have to stop to start,
in the mending of a broken heart.
Lose to gain,
in order to remain sane.
Die to live,
as you receive you must give.
Cry to laugh,
enjoy the second half.
You must work to play,
then find the better way.
Walk to ride,
take it all in stride.
Seek to discover,
be your own lover.
Then play the game,
and be ready for change.
You have to stop to go,
with everything you know.
Accept your pain
without fortune or fame.
Despair to hope,
learn how to cope.
Change your name
then move to a higher plane.
Fail in order to succeed,
a tender heart will bleed.
Surrender to fight,
live in the light.
After doubt comes faith,
find that better place.
From dim to bright,
Divine insight.
You must frown to smile,
be as humble as a child.
Sleep to awaken,
What is given must be taken.
Listen to be heard,
every single word.
Give in to transcend,
A spiritual blend.

DO YOU BELIEVE?

Some hath said as some now say,
the world will end on a given day.

Today is the future today is the past.
Do you believe the world will last?

Do you think it will end someday,
in a cataclysmic way?

Today is the someday our fore fathers talked about,
some with great hope, some with much doubt.

The "good ol' days" are here to stay.
what lies ahead is here today.

Stand firm on what you know,
the path leads where you need to go.

If you cannot trust yourself,
you will not trust anyone else.

What you need you will receive,
based on what you believe.

If you hope and never doubt,
you know what faith is all about.

LIMITATIONS and REALIZATIONS

Nothing - no one to blame.
Survival - the name of the game.
Give up what you must give,
do what you must do to live.

Slow down - stop time,
creatively explore your mind.
Dream - love - freely give,
no limitations as you live.

The only limits to what you can do,
are limits that others place on you.
Reach out into cosmic space,
there embrace, unlimited grace.

If the notion of God turns you off,
and my attitude seems much too soft;
accept me, love me, and respect me too,
I'll surely do the same for you.

I celebrate this defeat,
the lost of a political seat;
here is where I'm coming from,
"no attachment to any outcome."

Trusting completely, without doubt,
the correctness of how things turn out.
Knowing fully that all things are
working, as they should so far.

What have I learned from this?
Nothing at all, hit and miss.
There is more support out there
than I was even aware.

I received 56 votes.
Shocked I had that much support.
People are looking for a change,
sick and tired of political games.

I'm encouraged to hang in there.
There are lots of us who care.
Yes! the future is looking bright, everything will turn out right.

33

LIFE IS ...

Life is... we are...
We can wish upon a star.
Without a purpose, we can live
when we learn how to give.

Be glad for who you are,
when you wish upon a star.
When you learn how to give
then you'll know how to live.

Life so full, life so sweet
death can be a sweet retreat.
Oh to know.... to understand...
the secrets of immortal man.

Life transformed in time and space,
the universe our only place.
Two in one, one in two
you are me, I am you.

Deep... mysterious... under rate
highly over compensate.
Find the center, find the groove
see how the cosmos moves.

Joy and pleasure, pain and strife
all a part of cosmic life.
Learn to move into the pain
over and over and over again.

Learn to track... learn to measure...
equals out - pain and pleasure.
When you hurt, you must know
how and where you have to go.

When you do, what you should
you will know that life is good.
See the children of the night
always keep them in your sight.

Go to work... go to school...
sometimes you must play the fool.
Sound the alarm, remain calm
none of it can cause you harm.

Play the role, lose control
maintenance of your immoral soul.
Don't be shy, don't be bold
experience life as it unfolds.

SPIRIT OF THE UNIVERSE

Call her Goddess,
Call him God,
choose a name
take a part.

Ali, Buddha,
Mohammed, Jehovah,
whatever name
gets you over.

Mother Earth, Father Time
we must open up our minds.
With the spirit of the universe
we must learn to converse.

Find a way, learn to pray
this is a cosmic day.
Our intellect will connect,
the universe will protect.

Spirit of creation,
each day a celebration.
Today a variation
on the cosmic foundation.

Still the body, calm the mind,
a mystical connection you will find.
With the great cosmos get in tune,
we are born of this cosmic womb.

THE HIGHER SELF

For what I do, hire me, because I am good.
Sometimes I deal in fantasy, often misunderstood.
I always give all of me to get the job done,
and just because life is short, I have a lot of fun.

You ask me, "What do I do?" Well listen while I tell you!
I am a friend, I am a lover; I will help you to discover:
secrets in the universe, and all the things that you can trust.
Of life, I'll show you many sides and secret places where truth hides.

I am passion, I know lust, I know there is only us.
I know love, I know hate, most of all I can wait.
I am patience, I am truth, and know all the follies of youth.
I always was and always will be, I am infinity.

I am weak, I am strong, spinner of tales, singer of songs.
I search high, I search low, leading where we need to go.
Follow me as I lead, your hungry soul I will feed.
I have exactly what you need, to survive and to succeed.

I am there when you smile, just because I like your style.
I am there when you cry, and I'll be there when you die.
I am an invisible part of you, just look at the things we can do.
There are no limits on my mind; I'll take you beyond space and time.

Even beyond eternity, and show you what is meant to be.
I have an unlimited repertoire, together we can venture far.
You can be a tree, a rock, in time, ticking like a clock.
Traveling regions of the soul, far beyond the great black hole.

If you will only stick with me, the "Big Bang" you can see.
I'll show you what is yet to come, and places where it's coming from.

Of what I have, I give you some!

I'll give you all of me, for time and eternity.
If you but hire me, the Cosmos you will see.

BABY, BABY, BABY

Fast baby fast, and please don't smoke no grass.
Run baby run, try to stay out of the sun.
Dance baby dance, take a chance on romance.
Sing baby sing, and do your own thing.

Love baby love, and focus up above.
Hate baby hate, but you've still got to wait.
Go baby go, stand on what you know.
Turn baby turn, and use what you have learned.

Smile baby smile, then take it easy for a while.
Look baby look, until you find the hook.
See baby see, and find your destiny.
Swing baby swing, until your bell rings.

Pray baby pray, all night and day.
Ask baby ask, then complete the task.
Groove baby groove, until you make your move.
Lie baby lie, if you want to die.

Give baby give, if you want to live.
Share baby share, show how much you care.
Dare baby dare, receive the answer to your prayer.
Work baby work, and deal with the jerks.

Fly baby fly, until you reach the sky.
Shoot for the sun, and when you reach the moon,
in the course of time, it is not too soon;
you'll know that you are, a bright and shining star!

A MUSICAL MOTIVATION

When everything is going wrong,
let's find ourselves a happy song.

When we are down, sing along
we can hum it all day long.

We can lift our spirits high,
gravity we can defy.

Soar to places yet unknown,
Sewing seeds yet unsown.

Motivated musically,
Rhythm, soul and harmony.

Just to hear such lovely sounds,
is what we need to bring us 'round.

A single divine melody,
is sure to set our spirits free.

A PLACE INSIDE TO KNOW
(Written for contest supporting Multiple Sclerosis research)

Much of what I see in you reflects my own soul;
Uncontaminated truth, surely doth unfold.
Looking deep within myself, I can find you there;
Together we are one in God, infinity we share.
If I can find great love for you, you have what I desire;
Peace and joy I see in you, all things I admire.
Looking for someone to blame, I say it's you I hate;
Every time I see your face I say I can't relate.

So much of what I hate in you, I deny in me;
Closed off from my inner self, this I cannot see.
Love will always bring us back, where we need to be;
Everything I see in you is a part of me.
Relationship is divine, designed that we might grow;
Over into higher love, all things we might know.
Somehow each relationship, allows evolution;
Inside ourselves, we must go, to find each solution.
Search until you find, the inner divine; far more real than space or time.

38

III
personal growth

Vine Leaf

STRIKE A BALANCE

This is how I see myself,
split into separate parts;
one part ruled by my head,
and the other ruled by my heart.

There is a mature side to me,
I am also a little girl;
sometimes I'm a diamond in the rough,
at other times I'm a cultured pearl.

Most of the time I am very kind,
going that extra mile;
then again I am a distant friend,
giving not even a smile.

At times I'm cold, at times I'm hot,
very seldom am I the same;
most of the time I'll cooperate,
then again I won't even play the game.

Is there something wrong with me?
Is there a correct and normal way to be?
The fact that I even question myself
tells me, "I have lots of questions left."

I appear to be very sure of myself,
then again, I am so full of doubt.
Some days I am very content with my life,
other days I don't know what life's all about.

To strike a balance we need two sides,
sides that are opposite;
one that is good, one that is bad
from both sides we benefit.

To understand 'up,'
there must be 'down;'
to appreciate a 'smile,'
we must experience a 'frown.'

To comprehend 'go,'
we must understand 'stop;'
to hit the 'bottom,'
adds meaning to the 'top.'

When we experience 'soft,'
we learn the meaning of 'loud;'
from having been 'ashamed'
we learn the meaning of 'proud.'

This could go on and on
from time into eternity,
it brings balance to our existence
and expands relativity.

AGING

Two old ladies were talking
and one of them stated this well,
she looked at her friend and said,
"getting old is hell!"

Aging is real sneaky
for daily you can hardly tell,
then suddenly you realize
that, "getting old is hell!"

Comparatively speaking
you are probably still young,
but to even younger people,
it is with the old you are among.

How do you know when you are old
or, what is happening to you?
when one day you realize
there is nothing you can do.

As long as life is exciting,
there are lots of things to learn;
you need to remain open minded,
if aging is a big concern.

Time keeps on ticking,
nothing can make it stop.
Prestige, wealth nor fame,
affects the ticking of the clock.

Father Time is fair,
he treats us all the same;
but Mother Nature is tricky,
she plays a different game.

There is a point in time,
we stop to summarize;
and how we proceed from there,
separates the foolish from the wise.

It happens to you about mid-life,
and a crisis it can be;
things can get confused,
causing you to: doubt your stability,
    spout out profanity,
    develop a dependency,
    flee from reality, to
    live in a fantasy, then
question your sanity.

This is about the time
    you start to realize,
        you are getting older
            but maybe not so wise.

Then you look back on your life.
What do you see?
Did you use your resources wisely?
Are you all that you can be?

I openly admit
this is very hard for me,
for I am not real sure
I am all that I could be.

But, I am glad
for it gives me new goals,
and it also leaves me
with a longing in my soul.

I will always be learning
until the day I die.
I will strive to be honest
for I don't want to live a lie.

I will always be seeking
for truth and reality,
loving others, trusting God
for aging is my destiny.

WRITING POETRY

I am compelled to write
my thoughts and feelings down,
occasionally I write a melody
to give a poem melodic sound.

There are so many things
I would like to do and see,
like recording some of my songs
and publishing my poetry.

I love going out to speak
on subjects of interest to me,
it is very therapeutic
to express my feelings in poetry.

I think to myself,
if this is helping me,
I can pass it on to others,
in need of therapy.

The themes are universal
for feelings are all the same.
Circumstances and experiences may differ,
but pain is still pain.

Someone is always hurting
in one way or another,
that someone could be a friend,
a sister or a brother.

A father or a mother,
a co-worker on the job,
even supervisors
have occasions to sob.

I guess I will keep on writing
until the very end,
as I keep on learning,
on God alone to depend.

A CALLING

I love poetry,
I pray in rhyme,
I think in verse,
All the time.

Life itself
is a rhyme to me,
organized patterns
of poetry.

Sometimes life is music,
an exciting melodic line;
constantly stepping in rhythm,
occasionally marking time.

Could this be a calling,
"Writing poetry?"
It is a wonderful way
to capture reality!

For every poem I write,
contains a part of me;
calmly shared with others,
oh! so lovingly.

I am like a time bomb ticking,
I have so much to say;
I have to write a poem,
almost everyday.

FACING and EMBRACING PAIN

Physical pain and emotional pain
both can be a horrible thing.
It is something we all must face
and eventually we have to embrace.

Pain in the present,
triggers pain from the past.
If we don't face and embrace it,
this cycle will forever last.

We must stand firmly in God's grace,
and examine every painful detail face to face.
If we get angry, it is okay
and shedding tears is a perfect way;

to work through pain and get anger out.
This is what the healing process is all about.
Facing the tough stuff in the present and past,
embracing it and dealing with it at last.

A FRIENDLY REMINDER

At times
I don't want to cope,
I just want
to sit around and mope.

Have a pity party,
feel sorry for myself;
pretending it's all over,
and there is nothing left.

But it is not that easy,
for life goes on.
In the midst of solitude,
there is a ringing telephone.

A friendly reminder,
you are not alone;
a friendly voice greets you,
on the telephone.

It's the voice of God
sounding through a friend'
just a friendly reminder,
"self pity" is a sin.

So get yourself together,
remember: "life goes on."
You have a friendly reminder,
it is your telephone.

When you need to talk to God,
God is always there.
Let the phone remind you,
to talk to God in prayer.

GROWN - CHILDHOOD GONE!

When I was a young teen, it came to me
while picking cotton in a field, I could plainly see
that life could be better, with a college degree.

I didn't realize when I took the chance,
that the first thing to go would be romance,
I couldn't even party, I didn't have time to dance.

Earning a scholarship was a great reward,
it also meant I had to work very hard,
and with people and things I had to part.

I had to create a routine and discipline myself,
work until I had nothing left,
and I could not depend on anybody else.

This was a thing I had to go alone.
No more spending hours on the telephone.
My childhood was gone, and I was grown.

There was no silver platter held out to me,
no time to rest underneath a tree,
if I was going to graduate college successfully.

By the grace of God I came through,
at times I didn't know what I was going to do,
but I could always hear God saying, "I love you."

WHAT I DO

I am a poet, writer of poems.
I make music, singer of songs.

Though it may be offensive to you,
writing poems, singing songs,
that is what I do.

Sometimes I am driven, from deep down within.
I am a helper, I can be a friend.

I cannot stop, please don't ask me to,
writing poems, singing songs,
that is what I do.

You can ask me not to share them with you,
but writing and singing,
this I must do.

If you don't like what I do, maybe you don't like me.
I am music and poetry,
and they are me.

If you cannot accept me for myself,
you will have to find
somebody else.

I am learning to accept myself,
I feel good inside,
the spirit of love within me abides.

I will only change to suit my own taste,
within the framework
of God's amazing grace.

Who you are, and what you do,
I accept because, "I love you!"

HOLDING PATTERN

I am living in a holding pattern:

> Hating this waiting.
> Yearning and turning.
> Learning while journeying.

I exist in a holding pattern:

> Listening and glistening;
> looking, booking and cooking.
> Coasting and roasting,
> toasting and posting.

I work in a holding pattern:

> Heeding my reading.
> Needing and pleading.
> Seeding for feeding.
> Succeeding at leading.

I am growing in a holding pattern:

> Praying, obeying and staying.

I am living in a holding pattern!

STATE OF AFFAIRS

Where is hope in our world today?
When will our children learn to obey?
What is the role that we must play?
Renders one speechless, what can we say?

Where, my friend does the answer lie?
Failure means that we all will die!
This madness must someday come to an end.
Are we ready always, truth to defend?

Everything in our universe connects.
Every action's reaction reflects,
so why do we act so surprised,
when the truth is compromised?

We have to reap just what we sow.
Sometimes we don't know which way to go,
then we come full circle to how it is,
God as "her," and God as "his."

NOT FOR SALE

So much of my time I have sold,
and some I've given away;
but now I am all sold out,
and I'll not sell another moment, of another day.

I need some time for myself
away from a world confused.
Time to see myself,
some things do not amuse.

A paycheck must not determine,
which way my life will go.
There is a higher calling,
this one thing I know.

I've had to ask myself,
am I selfish and greedy,
or will I commit myself,
to the helpless and the needy?

There is no question left in my mind
the choice is plain to me,
for I am but a simple part
of time and eternity.

I AM NOT, I AM

I am not my job,
neither my career.
I know there is a reason,
that I am here.

I am not my race,
the color of my skin.
I am not my family,
neither am I my kin.

I am not my gender,
not even androgyny.
None of this is who I am,
none of this is me.

I am not my house,
nor my neighborhood.
I am not bad,
neither am I good.

I am not my car,
the one each day I drive.
I am not where I come from
neither where I arrive.

I am not my state,
I am not my town,
I am not my smile,
neither am I my frown.

Am I education?
No! I am not!
Neither am I knowledge,
or anything I've got.

I am not my wealth,
nor my poverty.
What I have or do not have,
has nothing to do with me.

I am not what I give away,
nor the things I Keep.
I am not what I eat.
nor my dreams when I sleep.

There is no label made for me,
that tells who I am;
and this is why I say to you,
"I am not, I am."

ALL MY CHILDREN

My poems - my children, the fruit of my womb,
my extension - my legacy, from beyond the tomb;
brought forth in pain and agony,
travailing in birth, brought forth from me.

My gift of love, my contribution,
to the world without retribution;
each poem unique, a fingerprint
each poem related - gives a hint.

As I live my life each day,
listening to what the children say;
constantly they speak,
of secrets I have tried to keep.

They speak of love, they speak of hate
they speak of hope; no it is not too late.
They speak of good, they speak of bad
they help me when I am feeling sad.

They speak the truth, they speak a lie
they'll live on though I must die.
They speak of right, they speak of wrong
with music they can become a song.

My children, my life, my legacy,
this each poem is to me.
I send them forth to help and heal,
as we surrender to divine will.

My children are my reality.
through them, God speaks to me.
Each poem I love as my child,
some are tame and some are wild.

ANIMUS

Nearest, dearest, newest friend
so much I want to say,
I am so glad to realize
loving you is the way.

Lovers, yes we will be
for lovers, we are;
trusting the transcendent power
protecting us so far.

I feel your being all around
both inside and out;
metaphysical experience
of this I have no doubt.

Amazing, splendid, fascinating
daily I experience you;
another part of myself
to which I must be true.

I know exactly who you are,
sweet masculine side;
I had you so sedated,
I thought that you had died.

But you got up to lead the way
to love, life and peace;
I wanted things to stay the same
mystery to increase.

But thank God, you did your part
took a risk with me;
and I'll be expressing my gratitude
throughout eternity.

FANTASY LOVE

"Fantasy love," oh so real
reflecting all that you feel,
"Fantasy love," like a dream
more than just what it seems.

"Fantasy love," will break through
to manifest itself in me and you.
"Fantasy love," cream of the crop
once you start you cannot stop.

There are emotions in my soul,
hidden things that cannot be told.
There is pain, oh so deep
causing my unconscious parts to weep.

Hating parts of myself
judging everybody else.
Ego resisting integration
In fact, demanding separation.

Fearing to trust the universe,
where there is no, "them," just "us."
The transcendent lurks in the dream,
ego stance to redeem.

From one extreme to the other
to love, to hate, one another;
grounding, balance, integration
beyond all contamination.

"Fantasy love," oh so real,
society's role is to kill;
who I am, who I was
this is what society does.

Caught in this double bind
locked here in space and time;
choosing to hold it all inside
praying it will all abide.

At times it wants to all break out,
and I just want to scream and shout;
then where I choose to find relief,
seems to cause me inner grief.

Based on what I've been taught,
and all of the "shit" that I have bought;
I don't know how to treat myself,
without love, what is left?

RESTLESSNESS

Integration
as
moderation,
moving
together
from
two
extremes;
a
message
spelled
out
for
me,
nightly
in
my
dreams.

AWAKEN BY GOD

The Spirit of the living God
wakes me up to write.
In time I have learned
to just give in without a fight.

No longer do I resist
the gift I have been given;
writing poetry for me
with passion I am driven.

Learning to stay in the moment,
in the here and now;
the God of love and life,
daily shows me how.

THE LONG POEM

Who am I now, who shall I be?
My soul, my spirit wants to be free.
Why do others want control,
of my mind, body and soul?

I am so glad of who I am,
and the things about which I give a damn;
things I do, things I did,
as an educator, I care for kids.

As a wife I am not too good,
not doing things that I should;
like cooking and cleaning or washing things,
I'd rather play piano sit and sing.

I love life, life loves me
there is so much on earth I'd like to see.
There are so many things I'd like to do,
some alone and some with you.

So many places I'd like to go,
bringing together friend and foe.
The only limits are in my mind,
they lock me here in space and time.

At times I want to just break out,
transcend all of my fears and doubts;
move up to a higher plain,
where there are no political games.

My life, an unconscious duplication,
of the parents of my procreation.
A saga of many mistakes made,
in this life, I have paid.

Trying to make things better, often makes them worse;
all part of some generational curse.
Sins of the father passed down to the son,
from mother to daughter until the battle is won.

This cycle only broken through divine intervention,
and readiness for divine comprehension;
otherwise agony will prevail,
each generation set up to fail.

Am I ready this cycle to break,
for body, spirit and soul sake?
Am I ready a risk to take,
and claim for me the life I make?

Do what I can, do what I could
and what I could I surely would;
sing my song, dance my dance,
Creating my own romance.

I knew I could, I know I can
gird my loins and take a stand,
then stand firm, myself and I
if I live, if I die.

Standing in the underworld,
as a woman, as a girl;
dare to face the great unknown,
sought and found my way back home.

AT LEAST ONE BOOK

There is at least one book in me
and I don't want to write it.

I don't want to be famous
and I don't want to be bold,
I just want to fulfill
the destiny of my soul.

I could care less if anyone knows my name,
I am perfectly happy without fortune or fame.

There are things about me that even I don't want to know,
and places in the universe where I don't want to go.

I like people and I like to be alone,
I really like to travel and I like to stay at home.

I believe in God and also in myself,
divinity and humanity there is nothing else.

Science and psychology religion and philosophy,
seeks to define destiny, somewhere beyond infinity.

I can hear the voice of God each and every day,
but at times I can't recognize, what She might do or say.

In life we cannot avoid experiencing opposites,
sometimes things work out, at times they just don't fit.

DOWN TIME

Rest, it's time, for I am tired.
Lightheaded, dizzy, rest required.
Feeling anger and rage inside,
my personal philosophy must not be applied.

Uniquely compared to nothing at all,
living behind this psychological wall.
I do not like what I feel and see.
that triggers this anger and rage in me.

"Chill out" my friend, this too shall pass.
Whatever is supposed to, will surely last.
And since I'm on this three day fast,
I'll live in the present, not the future or the past.

What is this anger that I feel?
Is this rage fake or real?
Sometimes we have to let it go,
and deal with things that we know.

Doubts and fears will not erase
things in life that we must face.
Productive is faith, amazing is grace
keeps us in the spiritual place.

It is always here and now.
Anxiety will not show us how.
To meditate is just to be,
eradicates anxiety.

I am so glad for this rest.
Easier to pass each new test.
Rest that helps ease the mind.
Thank God for "down time."

I AM

I am who I am, I am me.
You are who you are supposed to be.
I honor you and I honor me,
for I am who I'm supposed to be.

Yes, I honor who you are
but do you honor me?
On this I cannot speak
because this I cannot see.

I can only speak for me!

There are things
I do not understand,
but I accept
everything that I can.

The destiny of man!

"Mankind" that is
not the patriarchal "His,"
nor the matriarchal "Her"
if you prefer.

Just philosophical chatter
because it really does not matter,
silence versus clatter
lots of useless data.

The holy/unholy cheer,

"Where do we go from here?"

The answer is, "Nowhere!"
If you really give a care.

Because it's always here and now,
no one can show us how,
either we know or we don't
we can or we won't.

That's that! And I am still wearing my hat!

SMILE MAKER

When I'm sad and depressed, feeling a little down,
when I look in the mirror and see a frown,

When I need a lift, I use a flower;
then count my blessings in that very hour.

I say to myself, "You go girl,"
and put on my flower to face my world.

To celebrate life, I create a smile
even if I must cry for a while.

To remind myself, that life is short
I look through all of the shoes I have bought.

Some days I decide to mix and match,
from two different pair in my private batch;

to have fun with the kids and as a reminder to me,
that we cannot take life too seriously.

Sometimes I just don't like my hair,
so I have hats that will take me anywhere.

I collect jokes and funny little tales,
buy lots of junk at garage sales.

Some days I'll wear an African dress,
to celebrate my roots, I do my best.

I admit that I am different, and that's okay with me
though some may question my sanity.

Still I can only be,
the unique person that God made me.

I SAW ME

I saw me, on TV

> the good, the bad, the ugly.

I saw me, on the street

> with and without food to eat,
> shoes and no shoes upon my feet.

I saw me, in the face of a child

> uncontaminated for a little while,
> on my face a frown and a smile,
> with and without class or style.

I saw me, in your face

> standing still while running a race,
> without, within time and space
> seeking and finding my own place,
> within the realm of my God's grace.

I saw me, in a cloud

> very soft and very loud,
> alone in the midst of a crowd,
> very humble and very proud.

I saw me, in a book

> read and took a second look,
> searching for the psychic hook.

I saw me, in myself

> then I saw God - nothing else!

HOW YOU FEEL ABOUT YOU
(The Self-Inflicted Wound)

Message came, "You're not good enough,"
I said, "There must be something wrong with me."
Took this message inside myself,
and tried to shape my destiny.

Played the game, tried to change
to earn love and affection.
Lost my soul in a black hole,
then headed in the wrong direction.

For whatever reason, sometimes I want to cry;
I've felt so bad inside myself, I just wanted to die.
And I really don't know the reason why;
but somewhere inside, the answers lie.

Sometimes I want to scream out loud,
act out my pain,
then I stop and ask myself,
"What is there to gain?"

No one else can get close enough, to inflict this mortal wound;
that gapping hole in the soul, from childhood to the tomb.
We say, "We are the way we are," create the appropriate excuse;
learn to accept familiar pain, and so many forms of abuse.

Your weaknesses are my weaknesses, your strengths are my own.
And my weaknesses are your weaknesses, our strengths do atone.
But there is a path we each much walk, sometimes we walk alone;
on the road we discover, the path is leading home.

Nothing happens by accident, here in God's world.
We need each experience that we have, as our lives unfurl.
It's up to us to look beyond, and find the lesson there;
surrender to the Will of God, and find Him in a prayer.

We seek acceptance out there somewhere, where it cannot be found;
then we can't accept ourselves, when we get put down.
The instinctual need to belong, when greeted by rejection;
produces a more intense need, for love and affection.

There are answers and they lie, deep within the soul;
they are far, far more valuable, than the purest gold.
"Self acceptance," uncontaminated by anyone else's view,
are you in touch with yourself, "How do you feel about you?"

We must "let go" of everything else, if the soul is to heal;
to fill that hole, in the soul, and change the pain we feel.
We must accept our own true Self, allow others themselves to be,
only then can we find the key and live out our own destiny.

I COULD BE WRONG

Most of the time, I thought I was right,
then got a flash of divine insight!
And I'm making it the refrain to my song,

"When I know I'm right, I could be wrong."

For nobody can be right all the time,
Signifyin' and cryin' and lyin.'
Now I can add this verse to my song,

"When I'm pretty sure I'm right, I could be wrong."

I rant and rave when I think I'm right,
finding myself in verbal fights.
This short refrain, I am learning to sing,

"Girl, you can't be right about everything."

IV
relationship

A Touch of Night and Day

FALL OUT

Remember when you first fell in love?
Well, one day you might fall out!
When you are young, you are so sure of love,
but time can bring on doubt.

The very one you couldn't live without
could be the one who drives you nuts,
sometimes life gets boring
you must work to avoid life's ruts.

There is a stage of love
there is also a stage of hate.
Many times for love
it really can be too late.

I am in that stage of life
where love's labor is lost;
so I don't even try anymore
I don't want to pay the cost.

Mentally I try to prepare myself
to live my life alone;
I hate living in limbo
daily facing the unknown.

This is my lot in life,
"Be ready for anything."
Sooner or later,
for me the bell will ring.

NO PERFECT LIFE

There is no perfect husband,
there is no perfect wife;
there are no perfect children,
there is no perfect life.

Most of us are selfish,
wanting things to go our way;
seldom paying attention,
to what the other has to say.

We think to ourselves, "poor me,
my needs are not being met;
in this relationship,
what am I going to get?"

Oh! I want to be happy,
no matter what the cost;
even to the extent,
all else is lost.

What about love and virtue?
To thine own self be true!
I'll take care of me,
so you'd better take care of you.

When you first fall in love,
the other person means so much;
just a few days hence,
everything is dutch.

Sometimes getting dumped,
can be a blessing in disguise;
you can get past the pain,
if you are truly wise.

Even to hang in there,
daily amidst the pain;
can make you a better person,
if your faith remains.

There are two ways to view a problem,
two ways to suffer pain;
no matter how you view it,
the problem is the same.

But you can make a difference,
as you go along;
if you learn to harmonize,
adds beauty to your song.

You cannot control others,
what they feel or do;
the only control you have,
is that which relates to you.

So be ready to respond,
in a positive way;
to what others do,
and to what they say.

LOVED or LOST

If I am loved, shouldn't I know,
especially when I am told so?
But I am confused, don't understand,
I don't feel loved, and?

Feels like I am dying of emotional neglect,
I don't even know what to expect;
just feel empty and dry,
and I don't even know why.

It seems I have everything,
I surely have a wedding ring.
Can it be the flaw is in me?
I am loved but just cannot see.

Then what is wrong with me?
If love is so strong why can't I see?
Could it be love is for me,
and I am blind, unable to see?

As I think of love and count up the cost,
I think to myself, "I am lost."
Am I loved, or am I lost?
Like a salad, emotions tossed.

A FANTASY

There will come a man,
who will understand,
sexually what I need.

He will understand,
how to hold my hand,
my passion he will feed.

He won't have to wonder,
he will have my number,
caress me tenderly.

I will know his care,
for me, he will be there
he is my fantasy.

Where will I find,
this fantasy man of mine,
could he exist somewhere?

Because to me it seems,
he is only in my dreams.
Must I leave him there?

It would be nice,
as I think twice,
to have him here with me.

But he flies away,
with the light of day,
he loves so passionately.

A MAN'S TOUCH

A man put his hand on me,
and I decided to tell.
It was taken jokingly,
again my spirit fell.

It was not funny, yet I laughed
because I felt so small,
to realize no one cared
he was a friend after all.

It was hurtful to know, that friendship meant more
than any thought for me,
or how I felt about being touched
most inappropriately.

This experience brought back memories
of days from my childhood;
a very strange scenario,
I never really understood.

There was a man who was a friend
of my family;
who always tried when we were alone,
to touch and feel on me.

It was very strange to me
that it was dealt with as a joke;
just because he was adult,
and a good friend to my folk.

I spent a lot of time,
getting away from him;
'Cause anytime we were alone,
I knew I was out on a limb.

I leaned to fight and talk profane,
but learned how to save myself;
I also learned that I could not depend,
on anybody else.

The strangest thing, it was not discussed
the subject was taboo;
although it was unspeakable,
everybody knew.

People would casually say,
"that's just the way he is."
They just joked and laughed it off,
so many things he did.
In a flash this all came back,
when this man put his hand on me.
I knew before I said anything
it would be interrupted jokingly.
I admit the pain was the same,
it hurt all over again;
although over 30 years have passed
the fear felt the same.
Then not be taken seriously,
my emotions said, "dejavu;
nobody really gives a damn,
who cares what happens to you."
So this time, like back then
my anger directed inside;
but this time I recognized
my rage internalized.
He is a very likable man,
I like him very much;
God please help him understand,
my body he cannot touch.
Even to this very day
I jump whenever I'm touched;
to deal with a man's hand,
for me is too much.
So dear God I lift this up,
I know that you understand;
I pray your divine intervention
into the life of this man.
Now, like back then
trouble I don't want to make,
I handled it way back then
this should be a piece of cake.
Time will tell, we shall see
what shall become of this,
when or if it happens again
I'll be more than pissed.
Like all the times in my life
when I didn't know what to do,
I learned through prayer and faith
that God would see me through.

GOALS OF THE HEART

Looking back in retrospect----------------------------------things are plain to me.
Little did I know back then ---------------------------how things were meant to be.

In pain--I complained.
In pride---I lied.
Outwardly---I cried.
Even fate---I defied.
God knows--I tried.

Little did I know---but that I loved you so.
I could not overcome---so I called you a bum.
Insecurity---led me to jealousy,
that possessed my very soul------------------------------------then I lost control.

In fullness of time---myself I had to find.
First thing I had to do---was disconnect from you.
For years I did boast---that we were so close.
I had to face myself---there was no one else.

I had to disengage---to exit the stage.
My smile became a frown---------------------------------when the curtain went down.
My soul did interrupt--so I knew the jig was up.
You couldn't even breathe-------------------------------------for your Self I did seize.

You tried so hard to please----------------------------------and I wouldn't let you sneeze.
It all had to be---now both of us are free.
You are free to be you--I am free to be me.
Living on a new plateau---------------------------------------in peace as we come and go.

I love you today--in a new sort of way.
I know what to say---and I know how to pray.
Now we can grow---together, apart
each to pursue--goals of the heart.

INNER LONGING

I wonder what you feel for me;
to know, for me, is not to be.
I don't even think you know,
yet I love you so.

And really, that's okay,
it doesn't matter anyway;
as long as I know, what I feel
and my love for you is real.

I'm not attached to anything,
this old world seems to bring;
least of all to romance,
for I have learned the cosmic dance.

I am also learning how to sing
worlds apart, I've learned to swing;
in my heart and in my head,
things I know cannot be said.

More and more I comprehend,
sometimes we lose, sometimes we win.
In the scope of all eternity
what difference does it make for me?

The powerful force that we call life
is born of pleasure, pain and strife.
Life goes on with or without,
of this there is no doubt.

The cycle of life and death
passes with each cosmic breath;
and things are just as they should be,
I am you and you are me.

If I live a long, long time
what will I seek, what will I find?
Denying any part of me,
certainly will not set me free.

So, I am learning how to trust,
the universe is all of us;
together we are set apart,
each on a private search for God.

Passions and pleasures reach out to me
as I grow spiritually,
but I sigh and cross a leg,
then go to sleep when I go to bed.

CONFESSION

I have waited for so long
but now that you are near,
I can feel my heart palpitate
and I'm so full of fear.

Please! Please! Please slow down
you're taking me too fast,
I'm so afraid that what I've found
surely cannot last.

Although I know, that's okay
life holds no guarantee,
that what we find, we can keep
good things in life are free.

I need you and you need me,
I think that is enough.
Simple, without explanations
or other psychological stuff.

Your voice so sweet with sexy sounds,
music in my ears;
and it is that sexy sound,
that stirs up my doubts and fears.

You have done much for me
without a single touch.
I admit that I'm afraid
I like this all too much.

What good can come of this?
In time this too shall pass.
I get so disappointed
when things do not last.

Cognitively I know
this is how it must be.
The dance of life and death
is reality.

COSMIC PRAYER

God of love, God of life
God of all creation;
Help me now to make a choice
overcoming procrastination.

Help me accept this gift of love
if only for a moment.
Trusting in the universe
from whence all things are sent.

Help me give in return
all that I receive;
make me strong, where I am weak
in all that I believe.

-Amen-

SUNRISE

You are inspiration,
in lonely desperation.

You are a ray of hope,
I can hardly cope.

You are bright sunlight,
breaking forth at night.

You are peace and love,
sent down from up above.

At this point in time,
I'll think of you as mine.

So much to discover,
concealed in a lover.

I wonder what is next,
pure and simple sex?

There is nothing to be said
when a relationship is dead.

What a big surprise,
a new one will arise.

MEMORY

Living on a memory,
more exciting than reality;
expanding on that memory,
creation of a fantasy.

Things for me
as I want them to be;
disappointments and entanglements
of reality.

Active my imagination
all that's in my mind;
wherever I go, whatever I do
thinking 'bout you all the time.

How I suffer - deprivation
not one word from you.
Another hole, in my soul
and nothing that I can do.

This is good, this is bad
I am happy, I am sad.
Taking life very slow
whatever I do, wherever I go.

Although each day
my heart doth bleed;
this experience
is what I need.

Until I learn
and work it through,
this same work
I must do.

I think I'm learning
as I go;
some things I will
never know.

I want you, as you are.
You are what I need,
and in the fullness of time
passion will succeed.

SEX

No pretend,
no pretext,
pure and simple sex.

What has been,
we label as sin,
fits into the cosmic blend.

Fast count down,
erotic sounds,
smile into a frown.

Where to go,
where to hide,
holding it all inside.

Peace and love,
from up above,
fits together like hand in glove.

I feel good,
as I should,
I would tell you if I could.

(Smile)

You and me,
meant to be,
pure and simple ecstasy.

MUSIC

Your voice - music in my ears,
I am so glad that you are here,
I just want to hold you near.

It seems to have been so long,
each day I sing a brand new song,
it's to you my heart belongs.

You lit a fire in my soul,
now that I am growing old,
what I feel remains untold.

I just want to be with you,
I love all the things you do,
a transformation I'm going through;

Love so strong, love so sweet
what needs I have you can meet,
command performance, then repeat.

THIS LOVE

You keep popping up in my mind everyday,
affecting how I feel, what I do and say.
You will never know, because I will never tell
you are on my brain, ingrained in every cell.

I know that I'm the fool, yes; I'm a fool for you
because you offer me the things that I love to do.
I am to blame, my responsibility
what I feel for you started here in me.

What I project on to you, is the darker side of me
what I feel for you, is a love that is free.
Love with no strings attached, love that does not bond
love not limited to this life, "this love" goes beyond.

"This love" is healthy, "this love" pure and true
it is not related, to things we say and do.
This is a special love, a love pure and free
this kind of love will be around for eternity.

Love that supersedes everything we know,
it can dictate, places that we must go.
Some may call it lust, and lust it may be
for "this love" is everything, from sane to insanity.

There are no rules or limits, attached to "this love."
"This love" from down below, is also from above.
It makes no promises, there is no jealousy
no commitments, love completely free.

"This love" was in me, you brought it out
for that I thank you, and love you without a doubt.
I don't even know you, and don't need to know
fact is I need you, and I love you so.

Each time I see you, may be the last
true for everybody, as time, life will pass.
So I cherish each moment, I get to spend with you
enjoying what we share, what we say and do.

Spirit of creation, power divine
thank you for "this love," in my heart and mind.
Thanks to the little kid in me, my wild woman now is free;
free to love all mankind as I now love me.

PASSION

Passion can consume,
passion can devour;
passion that takes time,
giving pleasure by the hour.

Passion can be costly,
passion is complex;
this kind of passion,
is far more than sex.

It requires love,
it demands respect;
passion that discriminates,
is very much select.

It searches and it seeks,
until one day it finds;
the object of its affection,
passion is not blind.

Searching, looking, seeking
until it finds the best;
for this kind of passion,
settles for nothing less.

When the search is over,
and passion has her way;
there comes another call,
and passion must obey.

WEEP and WEPT

In offering you a part of me
that you could not accept,
this very tender part of me
sat down to weep and wept.

It seems you want a promise
that I cannot keep,
so that special part of me
must continue on to weep.

You want all of me
or none of me at all,
since this can never be
between us stands a wall.

To begin and end relationships
and know the reasons why,
even though we understand,
a part of us must die.

From this lonely place of death
we must quickly leave,
even as the heart and soul
continues on to grieve.

We must overcome
and move on in life,
even when the pain of truth
cuts just like a knife.

We must know what we need
our own needs to fulfill,
seeking, learning, knowing self
requires a special skill.

Things that I know I need
I know that I must find,
trusting in the universe
transcending space and time.

FEELINGS

Should I tell you honestly?
I wonder if I should reveal,
all that you mean to me
and all of what I feel?

Simple joy and adoration
deepest love profound;
I feel good about myself.
whenever you are around.

You bring out the best in me
with just a simple touch;
I never knew that knowing you
would come to mean so much.

Can I give back what I get?
I will if I can.
I've been blessed just knowing you
you are the dearest man.

From the first time that we met
you've been an inspiration,
in trying to do what is right
you are my motivation.

CHASING THE DREAM
(The Unfulfilled Woman)

To date, I have not met a man
who cares enough or understands;
what it really takes
female passions to awake.

Most of them are hot to trot
but satisfy, they cannot.
Even the arrogant gigolo
trust me, he does not know.

When the man is aroused
and puts his hand in your blouse;
what he is trying to do
has little or nothing to do with you.

You are just a human toy
to satisfy his need;
he'll say most anything
in order to succeed.

He thinks that it is fair
if you really care;
to let him have his way
submit and just obey.

There has to be a man who knows
how to curl a woman's toes;
fulfill her desire, satisfy her need
for more and more she will plead.

Sometimes the "shit" you read in books
only serves to get you hooked.
When all you need is just "good sex"
and everything that will come next,
for most men, this is too complex.

These things they will not talk about
because of fear and much self-doubt;
so, on and on the story goes
end of book, pages closed.

THE SOUL IN SEARCH OF MATE

Lonely, bored, wanting and sad,

searching for something never had,

at least not on this psychological plain,

needing to connect once again.

Yin to yang, opposites

come together, perfectly fit;

unhappy apart, separately placed

coexisting under infinite grace.

The soul will search until it finds

the mate who brings peace of mind.

When mate and mate are standing there

coniunctio -- answer to cosmic prayer.

Each one, a soul mate

this simply means we have to wait,

then we each must recognize,

that we ourselves are the prize.

FORGIVE ME

"Forgive," me for being born
with all of the hats that I have worn;
I guess I just don't understand
what it's like to be a man.
"Forgive me" for having a thought
and all of the philosophies that I have bought;
I really do not understand
the attitudes of the average man.
"Forgive me," for being me
with my own psychology;
no, I do not understand,
the closed opinions of the average man.
"Forgive me," for getting dressed
and trying so hard to do my best.
"Forgive me," for standing tall
each time that I stumble and fall.
"Forgive me," for being myself
excuse me, I have nothing else.
"Forgive me," for what I feel
and just trying to keep it real.
Why do I need to choose my words?
They do not relate to what is heard!
There are things I have to say
because I know no better way.
"Forgive me," for trusting you
in all the things that I do.
And how do the pleasures that I seek,
turn me into a common freak?
You've got your nerve to label me,
according to your own philosophy.
For your information I am pissed
and your main point, I missed.
"Forgive me," for saying "hello"
I guess you told me where to go.
A "nice person" I try to be,
but some things I cannot see.
"Forgive me," if I say, "goodbye."
I do not choose to live a lie.
I wish you could accept me as I am
but I can see that you don't really give a damn;
so be it, 'twas a good time,
I'll work on getting you out of my mind.

DO NOTHING

It seems that you don't care,
makes "no never mind" to you;
the stage that this relationship
is now going through.

I want to do something
but I don't know what to do;
so I will do nothing
and hope the same of you.

I am determined
this time, to stay
with the pain of rejection
today, somehow, someway.

Emotions rise within me
that make me want to cuddle;
this does not make me bold
instead it makes me subtle.

I throw out hints
in sly but sexy ways;
hoping for sweet foreplay
the romantic pre-sexual phase.

I guess you just don't get it,
does this mean you're dumb or smart?
You say come right out and tell you
but that's a damn bit hard.

Even if I tell you
you just don't "get it,"
then when we are finished
I hardly know we "did it."

I'd say, I'm in a pickle,
but God knows I ain't tickled.

Unsatisfied, frustrated
all things related.

What makes me so perplexed
is not just the act of sex;

there is so much more involved,
this problem I have not resolved.

So much time has passed,
yet the situation last.

No! This is not new
there is nothing for me to do;

of the things I have done,
nothing lost, nothing won.

One thing left for me to do,
admit that I am sad and blue.

I must have faith in myself,
not looking to anyone else.

Accept what life has for me
being all that I can be;

seeking help, where I can
trying my best to understand.

Life is hard but it is fair,
I must turn to God in prayer.

I'M OKAY BUT I AIN'T ALL THAT

Disgusted with myself yet, I say, "I'm cool,"
when the basic truth is, "I'm a damn big fool."
Transparent and vulnerable, bearing raw my soul,
the agony of rejection when the truth unfolded is told.

> I'm gonna stay with this pain, stand firm and let it hurt,
> even though facing it, makes me feel like dirt.
> What I seek outside of me, truly dwells within
> the fact that I am blind to it, is my greatest sin.

I cannot live this way, I cannot go on
a change has to come; I'm on my way back home.

~~~~~~

This restlessness is hell for me, drives me to the edge
and only to sobriety, will I make a pledge.

You see: I did the chasing, so I cannot complain,
this truth I am facing is causing me great pain;
but, I must grin and bear it, just embrace this pain
"a smile" I must wear it, and hope this never happens again.

> I am sad and depressed and yet great joy I know.
> The sad, sad story I can tell, is a tale of joy and woe.
> I am glad of everything in this life, I have come to know
> every tale of joy and love, and every tale of woe.

Everything in this world, resides here in me
as I learn how to face my own humanity.
The same question rises up, over and over again
where do I go from here, where have I already been?

PRESENT PROGRESSIVE

Back in the day, we found a way
to share something great.
At least, to me it seemed to be
remembering our first date.

Under the sun you were the one
who filled my every thought.
What I was to you, had much to do
with commodities sold and bought.

Now! I'm hurt feeling like dirt
with only myself to blame,
because looking to you, had little to do
with my psychological pain.

I know why we both deny
our plain and simple truth,
yet understand all we can
about the follies of our youth.

I needed you and you needed me
to fulfill a different need.
We were wrong, to just go along
neither to succeed.

Then to know and let it go
came easier for you.
Try to commit, to something legit
is what I have to do.

SOME MEN

Don't understand anything about women
And "for real" don't care,
not even willing to pay attention
or truly notice when we are there.

Some men see women as, "means to an end"
to keep them full and fed.
Satisfied in bed.
Listening to what is said.

A thing, a tool
A slave, a footstool.

Well, I say forget that, 'cause
I ain't no damn pussycat.
If this is how it has to be
you can all just forget about me.

I know that men are not all the same
a few choose not to play the game,
but they are few and far between
you might find one in a dream.

I tell you...for the most part
every one of them will break your heart.
You just have to face the pain,
for the cycle repeats again and again.

THIS POEM I WRITE

I desire peace,
I do not wish to fight;
living in tranquility,
this poem I write.

I am sad and lonely,
my spirit takes flight;
in my melancholy,
this poem I write.

Possessed by jealousy,
and things that cannot be;
from a second sight,
this poem I write.

Wherever love is found,
pain will abound;
in this cosmic light,
this poem I write.

Crazy as a loon,
in light of the full moon;
seem to be my plight,
therefore, this poem I write.

When I leave,
and don't come back;
because I might,
this poem I write.

Yes I know,
that it's too late;
of what I know,
you cannot wait.

You are you,
I am me;
this is how,
it is meant to be.

Don't complain,
life remains;
things can never,
stay the same.

We must let go,
and move on;
hear and now,
the final home.

THE FALL

From up there, to down here
from the ozone, to the atmosphere
from fantasy, to reality
life is still a mystery.

I actually begun a fairy tale life
when I became a legal wife;
because my tale was so very tall,
I experienced one hell of a fall.

I ascended, just to descend
full of air, a bag of wind
tried so hard my life to defend
upon a lie, my sanity did depend.

A hellish cycle, up and down
a heavenly cycle, earthward bound.
God fell from heaven, into my soul
the philosopher's stone, from lead to gold.

In this world of duality
time melts into eternity.
Eternity into infinity
where I am you and you are me;
for the most part, this we cannot see.

But it is true, when truth is told
that can be seen as life unfolds.
Acceptance is the name of the game
we must learn to accept everything.

Things that we do not understand
relationships between woman and man.
Projections outward, projections within
things we do not comprehend.

V
cultural/ethnic/gender

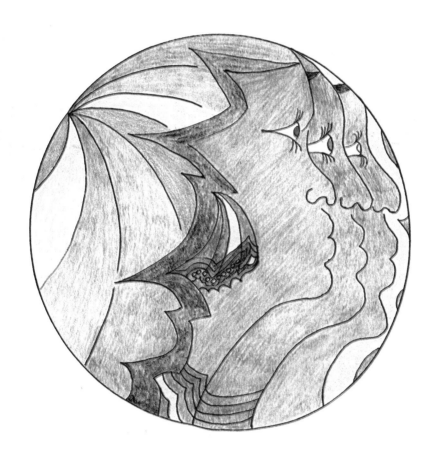

Women of Color

BLACK WOMEN BEWARE!

We deceive ourselves if we don't know
there is nothing at all to fear;
a lot going on in this world today
may cause us to shed a tear.

When we start to think this way,
we are ready to be deceived;
life can reveal so much deception,
that the truth is hard to believe.

Let me set your mind at ease
before I stereotype.
I will not condemn a race of people,
these few just happen to be white.

They have no conscience about what they do,
they must have the last say.
In the process they can ruin your life
take your job and your man away.

These women are threatened when we succeed
their jealousy rages out of control,
they know that they cannot compete
with the strength in a black woman's soul.

So the only hope that we have
is found in God alone,
He grants promotions on the job
and restores our happy homes.

Life can seem so simple at times,
we clearly know wrong from right;
so simple in fact, sometimes we say,
"it's as plain as black and white."

Life can be as simple as black and white,
but not in ways we think;
we may be thinking in shades of gray,
even brown, green, yellow, or pink.

Among the female gender
is a group that is treacherous,
they plot and scheme to get their way
making life hell for some of us.

Some black men are oh so weak,
stop thinking when they begin to feel,
losing control, over brain and soul
for just a temporary thrill.

Now we don't have the skill to fight,
in a way that is sure to win;
and when our emotions get the best of us,
it is hard for he brain to click in.

She is that strength within our souls,
from slavery it has been this way;
this die-hard breed, is bound to succeed
white women won't have the last say.

THE MINORITY RULE

If or when you get your foot in the door,
you must quickly learn to be an Oreo;
for nothing at all is known about us
and learning is not a must.

Don't fool yourself we don't make it to the top,
we come close, then we're made to stop.
The problem is, who's in control,
we can only change the color of our soul.

If for you, success is part of the game,
these things you should have known before you came.
If you didn't, you had better quickly learn,
if moving up the ladder is a real concern.

Who said anything about what is fair?
Bring up "equality," don't you dare!
Think about it, things don't change
pretty much they remain the same.

Almost everyone is out for him or herself
refusing to recognize anyone else,
discriminating in a high tech way
because we live in a modern day.

You must learn how to play your role,
it is all a part of growing old.
It takes time for you to realize,
it takes more time to make you wise.

CAN I BE AN OREO?

Here I stand age forty-two:
What on earth am I going to do?
Can inside I turn white as snow?
Can I successfully become an Oreo?

These questions, daily are plaguing me,
the answers determine what I will be.
Why did it take me so long to see,
that I would face these questions eventually?

The answers scare me inside.
How can I afford to decide?
When the answers are already a part of me,
What I am not, I cannot be.

To survive in this system successfully,
I'd be forced to live a lie;
and the things that make me truly me,
I'd have to learn to deny.

Again and again I keep asking myself,
"Can I be an Oreo?"
I keep on dancing around this point
when I know in my heart, the answer is "NO!"

I realize the implications of my "NO,"
in my heart it grieves me so;
the fact that Oreos we must be
is a sad commentary for this society.

A BLACK FEMALE AMERICAN

There are some things you must experience
in order to understand;
like being born black
in this particular land.

Looking at where we've come from,
looking at where we are,
where are we going?
In many ways, we have not come very far!

We have to admit that things are better, than they were in the past.
I wonder how much longer, inequality and bigotry will last.
There are rules and there are rules, a set for the majority,
there is a different set of rules, reserved for minorities.

Does any of this sound familiar, like a single violin string?
I know that it is not over, for the fat lady did not sing.
As usual we hang in there, even when it seems no one gives a care.
We know first hand, that life is not fair, but many of us believe in prayer.

Being black in this culture can be real tough; skin color can make things mighty rough.
No matter how much we do, it is not enough,
even when we know in our hearts we have the right stuff.

You can be stripped of your dignity, because your whole being just wants to be free.
If you haven't found out, take it from me; it is a sad thing to live in a fantasy.

Yet I am glad God made me black, and no one can make me take that back.
I am a black woman in this society, and in spite of my blackness and femininity,
I am free to be what God has called me to be, while maintaining my dignity,
working through the things that bother me, and for my life, taking full responsibility.

Accepting the good and the bad,
taking care of things that make me sad,
trusting God to take care of the rest,
life is a test, on which we must do our best.

We may be offered money in exchange for our soul,
to take it means we'll have to change our life's goal,
God never intended that to be,
and it is only in God that we can be free.

HUMAN DISGRACE

Nigger! Nigger! Nigger!
The lowest put down,
causes great pain,
just hearing that sound.

Affectionately nigger!
Reserved within our race,
a cultural expression,
and a saving grace.

Negrees! Supposed to be a step up,
but the intention is still corrupt.

Negro!
Linguistically defined,
attempts to place limits
on the spiritual mind.

Spades!
A term to defame,
all part of a cruel game.

Spooks and coons!
These nearly slipped my mind,
watch the older movies,
very little changes with time.

Colored people!
Encompasses a lot,
has something to do
with a sinister plot.

Black people!
Blacks!
Another name,
descriptive title change,
yet things remain the same.

African Americans!
What an interesting thought,
describing people
once sold and bought.

Racism is a human disgrace,
that people in this nation
just don't want to face.

IMPERFECTION

I am not perfect
neither are you,
we both can say
what we want to.

The U.S. constitution
does guarantee,
self-expression and speech
can both flow free.

You wish to place limits
on my constitutional rights,
the struggle for freedom
is a noble fight.

For I do have the right
my opinions to express,
though it may cause some
unpleasantness.

You may not like
what I have to say.
but I have a right
to say it anyway.

A statement honest,
factual and true;
apparently was
offensive to you.

It is okay
that we disagree,
you speak for you
I'll speak for me.

DOUBLE JEOPARDY

Black... in a white world,
life painfully unfurls.
A re-creation of what God made,
self destroyed, the price then paid.

A black woman... in a white man's world,
the same for every little black girl;
desperately trying to be herself,
if she fits, there is nothing left.

Trying hard to find her place,
predetermined by gender and race.
The name of the game is, "just survive,"
often it is, "just stay alive."

She knows rejection intimately,
her life a double jeopardy.
She must search to find herself,
identifying with no one else.

Life has dealt a heavy blow,
leaving her with no place to go;
so she finds a way to fit in,
self-abandoned just to win.

A great loss to the world,
the contribution of the "true" black girl;
for she has so much to give,
if only she were allowed to live.

FORGIVE and FORGET
(Politics)

White folk say, "Forgive and forget,"
but is that really fair?
Black folk have had to bear the load,
while living a dark nightmare.

Yes! White folk can so easily say,
"Forgive and forget."
We can "forgive," but not "forget"
on this you can bet.

White folk can afford to forget, because it's to their advantage,
Black folk cannot afford to forget, but some of us seem to manage.

White folk pretend all is well
and there is no bigotry,
as black folk we know how it feels
to be stripped of our dignity.

Equal opportunity
on paper sounds real good,
but there is no equality
when you grow up to live in the "hood."

Education, information,
developing the brain;
ignorance and poverty,
it's all a political game.

We criticize and judge the ones
who decided to just check out;
no understanding or empathizing with
what getting high is all about.

This is a crazy world,
the one in which we live;
where some believe it's better to get,
than it is to give.

Politics! Politics! Bittersweet retreat
Black or white rich or poor, success and defeat.

THE RACIST ME

Racists see through racist eyes
when they call us racist, don't be surprised.
They see the world from one point-of-view,
then point a finger at me and you.

There is no use in wasting time
trying to enlighten the racist mind.
After all, they do have the right
to reject universal insight.

Nothing they say and nothing they do
will put limits on my point-of-view;
for I have touched the universe,
and with the cosmos I am immersed.

I may not fully know who I am
but I do care and I give a damn;
about what life is all about,
of this fact I have no doubt.

Racism exists and always will.
It cannot be fixed with any pill.
Keep on singing, "We shall overcome,"
if you know where I am coming from!

SEGREGATION - INTEGRATION

Segregation is not all bad
although, it is not good,
neither is integration,
if we don't integrate like we should.

Where to point a finger
I really do not know.
Segregation, integration
two separate tales of woe.

I know that there is hope
and it is not too late,
for us as individuals
to individuate.

Skin color, a persona
just a mask we wear,
an accident of birth
of which we seem so much to care.

You are a fool
if you cannot see,
that skin color is an issue
in this society.

In the present and in the past
throughout history,
race has been an issue
defining wealth and poverty.

I wish that I could say
something wise and profound,
but everything that I say
puts me on shaky ground.

For I have had the experience,
of living in both worlds;
integration as an adult,
segregation as a girl.

Ask for my impressions, to tell you the truth;
I was most impressed, in the days of my youth.

At this very moment, nothing seems legit;
on days like today, I just want to quit.

TRUTH SELECT

Total and complete frustration,
working towards annihilation;
simultaneously staying afloat,
pedal point on one note.

Masculine to feminine masturbation,
feminine to masculine retaliation;
now we need a famous quote,
that we can recite by rote.

A cosmic form of constipation,
emotions now on probation;
though brought here on a boat,
we all get a chance to vote.

This is how the world is viewed,
when we all have been screwed;
on each other we project,
the skill to blame we perfect.

Continuing with the racial feud,
sexist remarks that are rude;
in the cosmos we connect,
if the truth we select.

LET IT GO and DRIVE REAL SLOW
(A southern traffic citation)

Situations in which whites can slide,
the letter of the law to blacks is applied.

Calibration and certification we cannot trust,
for the letter of the law is applied to us.

When I needed the experience of bigotry,
right up in your face;
God allowed me to travel,
to a distant place.

When we become a statistic in a southern state,
there are limits to the actions we can take.

The point is missed
when law enforcement gets pissed;
so get it right
before emotions take flight!

Pay attention, shut up, just slow down,
or from your flesh they will extract a pound.
Restitution for a mistake made,
comes only after you have prayed.

Let it go, give it up, keep moving on,
get the message, learn a lesson, and just go home.
Use the cruise, did not snooze, do your best,
if you pass, if you fail, it is just a test.

Once Upon A Time

Once upon a time, begins a fairy tale,
but there is also truth and meaning, in many others stories that we tell.
Stories distorted by pain and misery, stories about people who live in slavery.
Stories about human nature and the inhumanity of man;
how against cruelty and hatred, we must take a stand.

Learn about the history of your very own family;
who you are, how you came to be, this knowledge will set you free.
Slave masters, oppressors, very evil men
the thing that makes them evil, is not the color of their skin.

Learn from the past, about the struggle, the fight;
how integration of itself, cannot make things right.
Enlightened hearts, determined and bold; educate the mind, spirit and soul.
Develop and unfold!

What can this mean to you, young child, still in grade school?
Still learning to follow rules, nurtured and loved or labeled a fool.
You, like I, must learn to fly and touch the sky, before we die.
Answer the question, "Why?" Find a lot, in "Why not!"

It matters not the season, you were born for a reason.
Look inside and see, find your destiny.
Don't get trapped just to be, and then live on in slavery.
Real freedom, true liberation; comes with self-validation.

It matters not if you are black or white, this does not make you wrong or right.
It matters not if you're yellow or brown, tall and skinny or fat and round.
You will be judged by what you know and do not know, smart and witty or slow to go.
"The content of your character," is what Martin said,
not because of skin colored pink or red.

So don't you get to thinking anything just because you're...black, white; wrong, right;
yellow, brown; flat, round; red, pink; don't stink; boy, girl; in the world,
I hope you can, understand...?

As a member of the human race, in the cosmos, you have a place.
The whole purpose of your education is to find your sacred vocation.
Look to your ancestors, study your history; then perhaps you can see,
that this is the place, in time and space, where you are meant to be.

At school, they don't talk about God out loud,
but what you carry in your heart, you can be proud;
for God is the greatest part of our history,
it is Transcendent Power in the universe that sets our spirits free.

WHAT'S IN A NAME?

In the history of a nation, what's in a name, that makes you proud, or make you shame?

Call me a name that I don't like, and I guarantee, there is going to be a fight.
As a people we have so many names; had to learn to play so many games.
Now here is a trigger, white folk started calling us "nigger."

I can say, "You my nigger;" or "I'm yo' nigger." "Nigger" this, and "nigger" that!
But let a white person call me a **"nigger,"**
This I cannot handle, go on and call me a vandal; scandalize, vandalize,
there is shame, in that name.

Please join me in this refrain:
<u>In the history of this nation what's in a name, that makes you proud, or make you shame?</u>

With emancipation came liberation, in the name, a slight change.
We became the **"Negro Race,"** in America, sought to find our place.
Then Jim Crow laws brought segregation,
all **"colored people,"** had a separate station.
This is for "colored," that is for "white," 'cause black is wrong, and white is right.

Please join me again, in this refrain:
<u>In the history of this nation what's in a name, that makes you proud, or make you shame?</u>

When the Civil Rights Movement came, the time was right,
no more "colored people," now we were **"black."**
Black power, black pride, black is beautiful.
We even sang, "To be young, gifted, and black, that's where it's at."

Affirmative action, equal opportunity, just an illusion, even a blind man could see.
Now we march into century twenty-one, with all that has been said and done;
another change, in the name game, but are we free of toxic shame?

"African American," we are called today, what does it mean; what does it say
about attitudes, progress, and growth as a nation,
when so many still have a separate station?

Please join me in this final refrain:
<u>In the history of this nation what's in a name, that makes you proud, or make you shame?</u>

BLACK TRASH

Growing up, I felt like trash
my family had no available cash;
uneducated without decent jobs,
looked down on by cruel "black snobs."

White trash? Black trash!
It all feels the same; people are people; it's just a name.

People of color are biased, too
hurting each other in what we say and do.

Emancipation and civil rights,
basically dealt with black and white.

There is a deeper injustice, black on black
swept under the rug, afraid to look back.

White trash? Black trash!
What difference does it make?
What people do to people causes great heartache.

It has taught me to love one and all,
for who I am, to just stand tall.
I am learning not to judge by color of skin, not to judge at all
but trust God for knowledge to bring down the wall.

The wall that separates the human race,
truth about bigotry we all must face.
It comes in every color there is
the end result - silent tears.

White Trash? Black Trash!
It all feels the same, people are people, hard to explain,
we play stupid games.

mandala

Symbolic drawing, imagined or depicted.
Typically a circle enclosing a square. A pattern of existence.
Enclosure of sacred space and penetration to the sacred centre.

Beauty

A centre of power. Totality. Integration. Cosmic intelligence.
Universal spirit. The microcosm. Imago Mundi.
Pilgrimage of the soul.

INDEX OF POEMS

Title	Number in Collection	Date written
A Fantasy	505	08-23-92
A Man's Touch*	518	09-02-92
Goals of the Heart	737	04-05-94
Inner Longing	785	05-29-94
Confession	879	11-06-94
Sunrise	884	11-11-94
Memory	898	12-06-94
Sex	914	12-22-94
Music	927	01-10-95
This Love	962	04-02-95
Passion	1037	08-12-95
Weep and Wept	1042	09-02-95
Feelings	1048	09-25-95
Chasing The Dream (The Unfulfilled Woman)	1057	11-29-95
The Soul In Search Of Mate	1061	12-15-95
The Irony - (Forgive Me)	1076	02-16-96
Do Nothing	1120	03-09-97
I'm Okay, But I Ain't All That	1144	07-02-97
Present Progressive	1172	12-15-97
Some Men	1177	01-17-98
This Poem I Write	1185	05-09-98
The Fall	1242	04-09-99

Cultural/Ethnic/Gender Related

Title	Number in Collection	Date written
Black Women Beware!*	180	08-15-90
The Minority rule	201	08-29-90
Can I Be An Oreo?	203	08-30-90
A Black Female American*	343	06-27-91
Human Disgrace	521	09-19-92
Imperfection	573	03-25-93
Double Jeopardy	680	09-16-93
Forgive and Forger (Politics)	721	01-18-94
The Racist Me	725	01-26-94
Segregation - Integration	870	09-29-94
Truth Select	1045	09-14-95
Let It Go and Drive Real Slow	1314	10-23-01
Once Upon A time*	1326	01-21-02
What's In A Name?*	1333	02-19-02
Black Trash	1339	03-25-02

INDEX OF MANDALAS

ALPHABETICAL INDEX

111

Poet, musician, vocalist, motivational speaker,
story teller and artist.

Earned B.S. degree, 1969, Albany State University,
Albany, Georgia.

M.Ed. degree, 1976, and post graduate studies,
University of Toledo, Ohio.

Retired after 30 years in the field of education;
teacher, counselor, and administrator.
Toledo Public and Toledo Christian Schools

Served in the Ohio Air National Guard as
administrative specialist,
education training manager,
drug alcohol abuse control counselor.

Active in twelve step recovery program.

Currently serving as local church musician.
Performs poetry and music locally.

Lives in Perrysburg, Ohio, with husband,
Edgar E., retired school principal,
active member of the Ohio Air National Guard.
They have no children.